PLANNING
for WHEN

A Woman's Guide to Financial Planning

KEVIN W. PINKLEY AIFA®, CDFA™ CIMA®

The opinions voiced in this book are for general information only and not intended as specific advice or recommendations for any individual.

It is important that investors determine their tolerance for risk and their specific situation with a qualified advisor before making any investment decision.

Examples included in this book are for illustrative purposes only. There is no assurance that the objectives of any specific strategy will be attained. Consult the appropriate advisor for tax and legal advice.

Securities offered through LPL Financial, Member FINRA/SIPC

ISBN: 978-1-4834-4554-0 (sc)
ISBN: 978-1-4834-4555-7 (e)

Library of Congress Control Number: 2016901234

Lulu Publishing Services rev. date: 03/01/2016

To Mom and Dad for all the untold sacrifices. You taught me everything that is important.

To Elizabeth, Allison, and Josh. In you I see everything I have yet to become.

Contents

1

What's in a Name

SOMEONE SUGGESTED I COULDN'T use the original title I had for this book because the title painted quite a desperate picture—a situation some women find themselves in. It would have grabbed your attention and enticed you to read the book, which is the whole point of my wanting to pen my thoughts. Alas, I lost the battle, and the true title will never appear in print. But the good news is that my thoughts in the following chapters are unaltered, as they need to be.

Planning for When provides a needed course of action because *planning for when* is a requirement. So many times women are called upon to place others first. Be it biology, a nurturing spirit, motherhood, sacrifices for a relationship, or a gift from God, you've made choices to place yourself in a position of not being the most important person in your life. God bless you. No one else could do this in the capacity that you do.

However, you must not do it now, not with something as important as what we will be discussing.

My calling in life is to help clients prepare for and experience a retirement that helps provide a lifestyle that meets their needs and wants. In many cases, I help guide them in providing a legacy to a loved one or to a charitable institution long after they die.

In life, the things that disrupt this process include divorce and the loss of a spouse through death or disability. Sadly, divorce is all too common. According to CDC Divorce Statistics, the rate of divorce for first marriages is close to 41 percent. About 60 percent of second marriages end in divorce, as do roughly 73 percent of third marriages.

On that cheerful note, then things seem to get worse. Eventually time is up for all of us, and we depart this world, too often at the most unexpected point in our lives. Many of us, at some point, regardless of our situation, will experience the unexpected or expected loss of a spouse. None of us is immune to this.

Who was this book intended for? At the outset, it was for women who have found themselves, either from divorce or through the loss of a loved one, with the daunting and unfamiliar task of making financial decisions with very few options. This book is for them.

Through the process of putting my thoughts together, I've realized that women should seek this information before they're in that situation. My advice is not to wait until they're part of the intended readership of the book.

So here it is. No matter your circumstances or stage in life, you should read this book. After you've read it, you should hand it to your grandmother, mother, aunt, sister, daughter, or girlfriend. Don't mail it; leave it at their house, or even gift-wrap it. Hand it to them, and tell them to read it. It is that important.

2

My Goal for This Book

PEOPLE TELL US SETTING goals and acknowledging them is important. The people who say this are usually very successful. So here I go. My goal for *Planning for When* is to move you to complete a financial plan that will help to provide security and independence. When I hear this book helped to do just that, I'll smile and think, *Mission accomplished!* Since you're already reading this book, I know you're just the person who can make *Planning for When* happen.

3

Sometimes It's Better with Two

IF YOU AND YOUR partner have decided that being a couple is better than being an individual, take a deep breath and relax because you're halfway there.

As a couple, there likely have been times when you needed to sit together and find a solution to a problem or an issue that you didn't yet have an answer to or even a roadmap to address. Yet you acknowledged the issue together and decided to seek a solution. I'll bet most of the time it took input from both of you to resolve the problem; there were no easy answers. You probably felt better for bringing it up and committing to finding an answer, no matter how long it took.

The two of you need to *plan for when* in the same manner. You can do anything—together, that is.

4

My Husband Is Really Smart

CONGRATULATIONS. I HEAR THIS all the time.

I usually hear it when I ask, "What's your plan to continue in a lifestyle of security and independence, if and when your husband is no longer alive or not present in your life?"

Please notice I used the word *if* in relation to the unexpected happening at an unexpected time. I used the word *when* because eventually *when* happens.

So, back to "My husband is really smart." These women are trying to say that since he's really smart, of course they have a plan that will meet their needs. I hear that answer often because the wives do not know about the plan, if there is one, or if it will meet their needs. The truth is, usually there is no plan, and if there is, it's inadequate.

In case you're wondering, a spouse's occupation is irrelevant. To the point, the most woefully unprepared family I've met with had between them two master's degrees, a law degree, a PhD, and a CPA certification.

You must have a well-thought-out plan that meets your needs. Being really smart doesn't cut it. Being wise does, and there is a difference. Need an example? Try finding a biblical reference to the virtues of being really smart. Yet there are many references to a wise man. I will take wise over smart anytime.

Sometimes I think we use the term "really smart" to cover up for a trait someone lacks. Being smart with no plan won't insulate you from being really needy and dependent on others.

5

Why Men Act Like We Do

WHY DO MEN ACT as we do—that is, why do we not involve our spouses in financial decisions and planning? Some of my examples will be from observation; but some will be from my own past errors.

Men are notorious for not wanting to ask for directions if we're lost while driving. *We don't need any damn help! Who else would know better than us?* Call it ego or centuries of need and survival. The very trait that helped make us providers, hunters, and protectors sometimes works against us.

While genetics could be part of the reason for our behavior, I think that's a generous explanation. My belief is that, for most men, asking for help is a sign of weakness. Admitting that someone might be better suited at a task than we are—why, we just can't let that happen! If the solution didn't come from us, it can't be a very good solution, can it? Remember, we have to keep up the appearance that the man you married knows better than anyone else does. After all, aren't we in competition with everyone else?

Now, don't get me wrong. We understand we need help, but we don't want to face it. We have problems and issues with admitting we need help, and just getting to the point of admitting it requires overcoming huge obstacles. But once that happens, we've taken a big step toward improving the situation. By the way, we're going to need your help a little later with this very matter. If we were the only ones who suffered from our decisions, or lack thereof, that would be okay; however, our spouses and family are often left to answer for our faults.

6

Location, Location, Location

MY HOPE IS THAT by now you realize you need to have a conversation with your spouse. Perhaps *hope* isn't the correct word. I urge you to insist on it.

Wives need to have this conversation. The method I suggest for bringing it up may surprise you. You need to be thoughtful, tender, and considerate. If you aren't, you're going to hurt your husband's feelings.

I can't be more serious. You're going to make him feel vulnerable, perhaps even less than a perfect human. I'm speaking from experience and from my own observations. You may set off a series of reactions that are too varied and complicated to list. In summary, they will be expensive and unproductive.

You know the guy better than he knows himself, so choose an environment that puts him at ease, one that he's comfortable and familiar with. Go for a walk or to a baseball game. Flip through a family album together, go fishing, or have a date at the coffee shop. Don't ask questions at eight in the morning or first thing on Saturday after a frustrating week at the office. I also wouldn't suggest raising the issue as you're lying in bed about to go to dreamland or as he's walking in the door after spending an hour and a half in traffic. He can't handle it; he isn't like you. Just set aside time in advance so that it isn't pressured.

When the moment is right, ask, "Are we going to be okay financially should something happen to you? I need to know we're going to be okay. Tell me how we're going to be okay."

Now, here's the hard part: you don't want him to tell you at that moment. I know, I know. Just hear me out. What you're really asking is for him to acknowledge and agree that you really need to know in detail, not some glossed-over summary like "Don't worry. I'm a smart guy. We're going to be fine."

The two of you are going to set a meeting with your financial advisor and go over the details of your financial plan. In this meeting, you need to discuss where your plan is, what it's for, and how it works. At this point, you're probably going to find out there is no financial advisor and no financial plan. That's okay; it's why you had this conversation. We'll get to the point of getting an advisor and a plan a little later.

I am hesitant to say it, but there could be another scenario here. Maybe he just doesn't want to talk about it for whatever reason—plan or no plan. In a later chapter, we'll discuss what to do in this case.

7

Pushing Buttons

MOST OF US HAVE hot buttons that push us over the edge. A light switch goes off, and we can't think straight. They bother us that much.

You know what I'm talking about: pet peeves that we argue with our spouses over. If only they knew how much those issues bother us, they would knock it off. Here are some examples of these mind-altering problems. Even if they're not your issues, I think you'll get the point.

- Not returning the rented movie on time and being charged a penalty
- Forgetting to ask for the senior citizen discount
- Using an ATM other than your local bank's and getting charged a fee
- Not spending three hours booking plane tickets to save forty dollars

These things cause you grief and cost you money. Although you may find it hard to believe, they aren't the things keeping you from having a secure and comfortable lifestyle. If you're not *planning for when*, saving a few bucks on these hot-button items won't save you when something really big happens.

Don't waste time on these trivial things. Instead, focus on the life-altering changes that could take place. Imagine the feeling of dread you'd get if you had real concerns:

- No more paychecks
- The loss of your home
- A lack of funds for your kids to start or finish their chosen paths of higher education
- The inability to pay for needed medical care
- Your accounts only having enough money for just a few more months

Don't sweat the small stuff. Don't be someone who has no plan for when. *When* will happen; it's just not at the same time for everyone.

8

Guess It Wasn't in the Budget

IN THIS STORY, I will leave out the husband's occupation, but if you know such a person, you'll figure it out.

This couple had a lovely family with four children. The husband was successful and advancing in his field. The wife had a college degree and had worked outside the home prior to the children being born. Later she decided to focus on the children and not work outside the home.

With the husband's occupation, it was only natural and expected that they had a budget. There was a budget for the house, monthly expenses, utilities, gas, food, cable, vacations (planned three years in advance), clothes, hobbies, car insurance, entertainment, and pets. All right, you get the picture. So what was the issue? Budgeting is perfectly reasonable and necessary. I will give you that one ... maybe. Their budgets were very detailed, broken down weekly by category and item. This guy had a spreadsheet for laundry detergent two years out, with a history of the previous eight years.

When this forty-year-old husband and father was found dead on the bathroom floor from a heart attack, it was a terrible shock. He had no family history of heart disease and had made an effort to eat right and exercise. There was not, however, a plan to take care of his family when this happened. We know that everyone dies sometime, but in his case, it was far too soon.

Although this family was successful and living a comfortable lifestyle, without his substantial paycheck, they couldn't make ends meet. The house was lost, and the wife had to find a job immediately, and it in no way met the family's needs. This much-needed job took her out of the kids' lives from seven in the morning until seven at night, when she picked the kids up from daycare. The remaining time with them was spent getting them fed, bathed, and off to bed to start the process all over again.

The plans for the kids to attend the same universities as their parents were out the window. Of course, family and friends helped. There were collections at the church, raffles, and sales of chopped beef sandwiches. Yet it wasn't enough.

They had the means, background, and attention to detail. They just didn't have a plan.

9

What It Doesn't Mean

HERE'S ANOTHER SCENARIO: YOU sought the proper advice and had a plan that met your needs. Now you're filthy rich; you have a life of excess and indulgence. You're jet setting across the world with your new boyfriend, who is more than happy to help you spend your money.

Well, I guess this could be the case, but it would just require having a master plan in place. Of course, a plan such as this would require a large sum of money to fund it.

This scenario is usually what your spouse envisions and is a contributing factor to why a plan *isn't* in place. What I'm trying to convey here is that this is probably not your plan. Your plan should meet your needs, provide a level of security, and provide for varying needs. Those needs can be funded at a nominal cost.

As a person with large sums of money, you will need to work closely with your financial advisor moving forward. Unfortunately, wealthy people can and do outlive their funds, regardless of how plentiful they are or how they were amassed.

This is one reason you need to have a working relationship with your financial advisor before the unexpected happens. Having to deal with the unexpected or expected loss of your spouse is not the ideal time to make the acquaintance of the financial advisor your spouse has been working with for years.

10

Going Spartan

YOU MAY THINK THAT *planning for when* is overrated. After all, planning and creating solutions takes time and costs money. You may think you can make it without this planning.

You may think you don't need to have the lifestyle you currently have. You can sell the house and save money on taxes by moving to a different school district. The kids will just have to adjust. It would be good for them to struggle with college costs; it would build the character needed for hard times. Never mind that only about half of all the students who enroll in college graduate. Oh yeah, not being burdened with helping financially would be a good thing. Skipping those wedding costs for your daughter would make you feel good about myself.

Bull! Thinking you can survive financially for decades as things are now is utter nonsense. I could go into great detail about cost-of-living increases, the consumer price index, interest rates, the fed and treasury rates. However, that stuff is boring, not to the point, and quite possibly won't matter. *Planning for When* can help you provide financially for those who matter the most.

11

Ketchup and Crown Molding

OKAY, NOW WE'LL HIT on a subject that's sometimes touchy. A home is viewed as a reflection of you, and I guess to some degree that's true and acceptable. Most folks want to live in a home that's in a safe neighborhood, where they're comfortable in their surroundings. And if they have children, it's nice to live near good schools.

However, let us admit that sometimes we go way beyond these reasonable desires, and this is where the trouble lies. Having too much of your net worth and time in your home is a risk you might want to reconsider. Did you notice I mentioned having too much net worth and time invested? We'll get to net worth later; for now, let's talk about the time factor.

I'll wager you've spent more time picking out granite counter tops than you have on your financial and estate plan. How many trips did you make to the showroom? How much time did you spend shopping online? How many times did you look at your neighbors' counters, talk to your friends, and compare costs of contractors? The above-mentioned activities can be fun, but they're just not important. Don't sacrifice your well-being because of your surroundings. Now reread the title of this chapter. I hope you got the point.

12

Rolling Pennies

WE'RE WORKING ON SOMETHING important … like taxes. I choose taxes, but it could be any number of things. However, I brought it up, so here we go.

There are some important issues and different strategies to consider regarding taxes when purchasing or selling a business, inheriting an estate, or planning an estate. These important considerations are for people dealing in figures with plenty of zeros. I'm talking about people with large estates who already have completed their *planning for when*. Remember, you haven't done so. You and your spouse are wasting time and effort on something of little importance.

You don't like to pay taxes; in fact, you hate to pay taxes. Therefore, you search for an investment that you've changed in three of the last five years. You have a detailed spreadsheet that shows you saved $361.27 over the last three years. Maybe you did or maybe you didn't (another topic of discussion). You have itemized deductions of $18.03, $3.81, $54.37, $27.89, and $ 116.54. Every year you protest your property taxes. Sometimes you even hire someone to protest them for you. It's worth it because last year you saved $437.19. You aren't going to let them stick it to you! Don't worry; you're doing a good enough job of that yourself.

With the exceptions of the truly important tax examples at the start of the chapter, what you've been working on won't help you. Let me fill you in on a little secret: these are trivial concerns, and I use the word *trivial* because I can't use the word I really want to. These concerns don't make you wealthy; the numbers just don't add up fast enough. Working on these trivial items might make you feel better for a short period, but if you really think about it honestly, that feeling is soon lost.

Therefore, trivial concerns won't make you wealthy; and, more importantly, they won't keep you secure. Savings on taxes won't keep you in the home that you now can't afford. Shopping on tax-free weekends and itemized deductions won't keep you in your current lifestyle, provide for a loved one who requires long-term care, or help to fund a needed education.

You might as well start rolling pennies. Even as a kid, I hated rolling pennies. You know, coffee cans full of pennies. It takes a lot of time to count and roll them. Just try to buy anything that will help sustain you with one of those rolls. Pennies don't go very far. That was true forty years ago, and it is especially true now. Folks will never say they got wealthy with the money they saved on taxes. More importantly, you won't be able to sustain yourself and your loved ones with what you saved on taxes.

Yes, I'll admit saving on taxes is a good thing, but don't let it replace completing the really important tasks, like *planning for when.*

13

Someone Else's Well Always Runs Dry

WE KID OURSELVES TO think problems happen to someone else; in reality, we can only hope we aren't met with life's challenges. We think if some challenge does come our way, we can just rely on someone else to take care of us.

This far into the book, you might notice a theme. You might think it's about being unwilling to plan and face reality. Yes, that's part of it; however, I think there's more. We might not want to face it, but to some degree, we're relying on someone else to rescue us when something happens. We can't do this when it pertains to our family's welfare. Yes, we are social beings who want and need to be part of a group that learns to share and to trust others. We just can't rely on and trust others to make the needed plans without our participation.

By now, you're probably waiting for more examples. Well, I won't disappoint you. I live near the Texas coast, and every once in a while a hurricane bears down on us. Each hurricane always seems to be bigger than the last one. Floods destroy areas that survived countless other storms. In the aftermath, we're hard-pressed to find water, food, gas, batteries, diapers, and other needed items. We have to plan for the untimely or unexpected event that, by the way, always comes around.

During these storms, local, state, and federal assistance services are overwhelmed, understocked, and understaffed. It's the same whether it's in Texas or Louisiana or South Carolina. This isn't a recent phenomenon.

It has probably always been this way. We just think it's new and different because it affects us—and we're special.

I have a friend who grew up in South Dakota in the 1940s. Farmers and ranchers made that country their home. They were usually hardy and self-reliant, but sometimes they had to rely on others, at times to their regret.

A certain organization collected money from local families with the intention of it being used during blizzards to get much-needed food and supplies to the farmers and ranchers by plane if a blizzard snowed them in. So a couple of times a year, collections were made at the local schools. All the children would line up with their dimes in hand. And in those days, dimes were hard to come by.

The blizzard of 1949 was one of the worst on record, and the locals still talk about it. Farmers and ranchers were snowed in for months. The people and livestock were running out of food and supplies. My friend's family relied on pancakes because just about everything else was used up. Being of German descent, her most vivid memory of the blizzard was crying and saying, "No more pfannkuchens! No more pfannkuchens!" (*Pfannkuchens* is German for *pancakes*.)

Unfortunately, the plane never came to drop supplies to the desperate families. The families were on their own, much to their surprise. Today's farmers and ranchers are often reminded of this story. You can't rely on others; you must be self-sufficient.

14

Upgrades

AFTER YOUR FIRST MEANINGFUL employment, what happened? Things changed; you upgraded your car, your wardrobe, and maybe even your residence. After promotions and pay raises, did you start or expand a business? Then what? Upgrade the car again, vacations, a second home?

When changes take place, you must upgrade your *plan for when* as well. It isn't a once-and-done event. The commitment to care for yourself and your loved ones can change over time. Just as your salary from twenty years ago is probably not meeting the needs of today, that plan from twenty years ago probably needs an honest second look to see if it needs upgrading.

You begin as a couple, and if you decide to have a family, you have new and ever-increasing responsibilities and expenses. In summary, you're helping to provide for others. Sometimes this could include opportunities that you yourself didn't have. Those opportunities are important enough that you want to be able to provide them for your loved ones. You want the opportunity to care for your family long after you're gone. As your responsibilities and commitments change, your *plan for when* must change as well.

15

How Many Roofs Can You Afford?

CONGRATULATIONS! YOU PLANNED, SAVED, and sacrificed. Now you can enjoy those plans together. Just one question: did you plan to live under separate roofs? You might answer, "No, we didn't; we're a loving couple, and we want to spend our lives together." Well, you can, and you will. Just keep that in the back of your mind that you may outlive your spouse.

Something else can happen as we age. Sometimes we lose the ability to care for ourselves physically and mentally. I know that if this happens to you, you'll take care of your husband at home. Being the person you are, I wouldn't expect anything else. And you should do that, if it's physically possible. You can care for him, and you can get help so he can stay in your home.

However, you need to be very honest with yourself. Is your home set up to handle your husband if he were no longer under his own power? Here are some things to consider:

- Is the master bedroom downstairs?
- Will a wheelchair fit through your hallways and doorways?
- Are the bathrooms accessible for a wheelchair or walker?
- Can you lift your spouse off the toilet or out of bed without hurting him or you?

You might be able to provide some care at home, but many cases of disability require twenty-four-hour care and renovating your home to accommodate the new requirements. What about dementia or some other debilitating mental disease? You'll be dealing with a person who has limited cognition in an adult body. You can't leave this person alone. Leaving him to his own resources would be a recipe for disaster.

At some point, you might need to find professional, twenty-four-hour care; this means some type of nursing facility. Please listen very carefully and then read this one more time: You aren't abandoning him. You aren't violating your wedding vows. This change is for his well-being as well as for yours.

Even if you make modifications to your home and hire in-home care, you eventually will wear yourself out mentally and physically. And who will care for your spouse if you *both* need help? What a fine pickle you will both be in!

You have to take care of yourself so you can take care of him. You need to do this by seeking professional care. A study from the US Department of Health and Human Services found that 70 percent of people age sixty-five or older will need long-term care services at some point in their lifetime. The study also mentioned that the cost of help could range from $3,000 to $10,000 per month, depending on the level of care and the area of the country you live in.

Since we're talking about what tends to happen, let's leave nothing out. What I mentioned has a very good chance of affecting you and your spouse. I truly hope it doesn't happen, but let's not rely only on good intentions. The rest of the story is that while these changes are occurring, enormous expenses are being accrued, drastically reducing an income for you. The money you have to care for you and your spouse is quickly evaporating, and planning probably didn't include living under two roofs and all the expenses that go along with that.

You will be left with considerably fewer means to provide for yourself than you expected. You will begin to wonder if you're going to outlive your money. What if, at the same time, you require some kind of ongoing care yourself? There is probably just not enough money to take care of your needs as well.

You need to get ahead of this situation. Don't wait until you're seeing this happen to friends in your age group or you're experiencing it yourself. If you wait until then, it will probably be too late because there is a window of opportunity and a cost. If you address the need earlier, you'll have many more options at a lower cost. It will be more expensive to provide this care later, and you have the opportunity to leverage your dollars now for maximum benefit.

Okay, you acknowledge the need, and you want to have the most options at the lowest cost available. So what's the answer? Find yourself a caring, understanding, and knowledgeable financial advisor. Did you notice I listed caring and understanding first and second? It wasn't by accident. You might not realize how important these two qualities are until you find yourself in the previously mentioned situation.

16

If You're in Charge

AN IDEA CAME TO me while driving home one evening: I was failing to address a very important topic with you. You might have chosen to be without a significant other in your life. If so, good for you! You're in charge. On the other hand, through no fault of your own, you find yourself alone. Those circumstances don't mean you should put the book down and move on. You still have some decisions to make, and you need to act on them. You just don't have to convince anyone other than yourself.

Earlier we spoke of planning for a loved one's health care. Now we're going to talk just about you. Whether you have a family of loved ones or not, the following applies: You need to do some serious, deep thinking on who will make decisions for you if you become incapacitated and unable to make decisions for yourself. This person could be any adult who cares about you. He or she will be making decisions that you would normally make for yourself.

Oh yeah, the other requirement is that you have good reason to trust that person. He or she may be making some very important health care and final life decisions on your behalf. Don't neglect this important process. The news is too full of tragic examples of people with very different ideas fighting over what is best for another person.

You're too busy to deal with this? I hear you. You're being pulled in so many different directions. But save that excuse for someone else. Get this done immediately; it absolutely can't wait. Set a date and meet with an estate-planning attorney. You have to move yourself to the front of the line this time.

17

What's Most Important?

I HESITATED TO INCLUDE this chapter; however, just the other day I was reminded of what's important: physical, mental, and spiritual health. Different but interconnected aspects of your health must be recognized and addressed.

Find activities that help keep you healthy, recharged, balanced, and social. Being social is included because we are pack animals. Now, don't get me wrong. I cherish my alone time—probably too much. However, it's easy to become a shut-in, especially as we age. And I haven't heard of very many hermits who are balanced and mentally sharp. Being around other people is important. I mention activities in the plural because if you have only one activity, eventually you'll become bored, and you might stop your only activity. Don't underestimate the process of learning and enjoying something new.

Now, what's needed? *Planning for when.* It's just that. No more. No less. It's just needed. The goal isn't to need your plan until you have lived a long and meaningful life, then the plan takes care of when. If the unexpected happens, your loved ones will realize how much you cared for them. We just don't want to speed up the process because you aren't taking care of yourself and have to focus on the urgent rather than the important.

Here are some examples of what is *not* important. How about getting up at four thirty in the morning seven days a week to check your online accounts? Are you getting up every day at four thirty to exercise? No one needs to check accounts every day, and especially not at four thirty. You don't need to because you have a plan, and it isn't dependent on which way the financial or political winds are blowing on any given day. Neither is having your super-duper custom spreadsheet with five different colors that track the real-time movements of the markets.

What? you may be thinking. *Of course, this needs to be done. You're joking, right? I need to do this to remain in control.* Let me help you out here. If you're doing this, *you're not in control.* You're being bounced around like a rudderless ship in a storm—not to mention what this nonsense is doing to your emotions and blood pressure. The same can be said of listening to too much talk radio, 24/7 news, or nonstop updates on your social media. If you're doing that, you aren't in control, and you aren't doing anything worthwhile. If anything, you're using them as an excuse for not doing anything worthwhile.

Since we're on the subject of doing something worthwhile, I sometimes hear about people who avoid what they would call work, tasks, or anything that requires effort. After all, they're retired. Well, I have a question: just what are you going to be doing when you're not doing anything—probably not doing anything that is both mentally and physically challenging? This, by the way, is good for you. When you're doing something good for you, that's the good life.

The point I'm trying to make here is that you must take care of yourself. All of the hard work and time you put into being successful will be for naught if you're not here to enjoy the success. Take care of yourself and find the right financial advisor. Together you can build your financial plan, which is kind of like planting trees. You plant, water, feed, and nurture them. When needed, you do minor pruning. Most importantly, once your trees are in place, you basically leave them alone and let them take care of the rest.

18

Put Yourself in the Picture

SOMETIMES GETTING OUT OF your comfort zone is a good thing. One afternoon, on a gorgeous spring day at the park, I noticed two women out to enjoy the nice day and take some photos of the surroundings. One of them, the subject, moved from scene to scene, while the other took the pictures. The first, whom I'll refer to as the model, was dressed for the part, and I must say she was an attractive young woman. She seemed to enjoy her role, and it seemed to be quite natural for her to be the subject. But I sensed she wasn't fully at ease with her role. I'm not a photographer and certainly not a model, so I'm not speaking from experience.

What I observed was someone who knew what to do but wasn't comfortable doing it, yet she was the focus of that day's photos. The other woman was dressed in blue jeans and a long-sleeved work shirt. She carried a camera bag and a very professional-looking camera.

Yet if the model was attractive, the photographer was stunning. You would be hard-pressed to find a more photogenic person. She seemed at ease and moved with confidence. The model had a rehearsed look, and the photographer was so involved in the photo shoot, she didn't notice what was so obvious to me.

Later the model walked off, and the photographer was left snapping scenery and checking the lighting. I couldn't help but wonder why the photographer wasn't the model. As I said, she was an absolutely stunning young woman but, more importantly, at ease and confident. I wondered about their roles and if the photographer had ever considered a change of roles. It seemed like such a lost opportunity.

While sitting there, I was thinking, *If only someone would ask why she isn't the model.* Then I remembered why I was writing this book. So, off I went to have a conversation at the risk of coming off as a guy complimenting a young woman in the hopes of ending up with her phone number.

As I walked up to her, I was thinking of what to say or ask to convince her to expand her role. What I settled on was asking if she had ever considered being in the pictures. I received a confident smile from someone who was so at peace with herself that a stranger asking such a question didn't catch her off guard.

But what came next took me by surprise, and I fear her answer is far too common. She said she'd never considered it. Her older sister, the one she was photographing, had always wanted to be a model. And their family's focus was helping the would-be model to achieve her goal. Her role as the photographer was necessary to support her sister.

As she explained their story in detail, at no point in our lengthy conversation did she answer the question with something like "No, I couldn't. I'm not the model type. Do you really think so?" She had never considered it, but she had no doubts that what she was doing was the right thing to do.

After hearing her story, I thanked her for the explanation and asked a pardon for intruding. I didn't ask the question a second time. I felt there was no need to. She felt she needed to be in a supportive role to help a loved one and was willing to sacrifice for another. Yet she had great confidence that she would find her own way when she was ready. So, off I went, feeling better having asked the question.

Months later, I rode through the same park and observed the two sisters again. The photographer had transformed her confidence into action: she was now the subject of the photographs.

19

The Rule of Three

I TRY TO SPEND as much time outdoors as possible because I feel the most at home and comfortable there. When outdoors, unexpected things can and do happen. This doesn't keep me from enjoying it or make me afraid to venture out. I have, instead, spent time and effort in planning for something unexpected that may occur. One of the first things I learned from being outdoors is the Rule of Three. It goes like this: you can go three minutes without air, three days without water, and three weeks without food. This rule can also help you focus on accessing and managing priorities.

Folks who have explored caves or gone scuba diving at night always have three light sources. This sounds like overkill until you can't find your light, drop it, break it, or have it suddenly stop working. What you experience next is sudden, overwhelming dread and panic due to your loss of control in that darkness. However, if you brought another light source, you just carry on.

The essential Rule of Three in *planning for when* is to know where it is, to know why it's there, and to know what it's for.

20

A Candle or a Windmill

A FINANCIAL PLAN IS meant to meet your needs—expected and unexpected, immediate and future. It also should provide a controllable, renewable, and increasing income stream. Let me say that again: controllable, renewable, and increasing income stream.

Sometimes the financial services industry makes things so complicated they aren't understandable. Companies spend untold amounts of money to produce complicated charts, graphs, and articles with language and terminology that doesn't make sense. It rarely explains what is important. I will sum it up right here: you need to give yourself a pay raise during retirement.

Retirement doesn't work the way so many people imagine. Your cost of living actually increases. How can that be? The house will be paid for. You won't be buying any new cars. You'll eat leftovers. No commute. No dry-cleaning bills. You'll just spend less.

No, you won't. Every time you stand in the checkout line or shop online, you will encounter ever-increasing costs.

I have yet to meet a couple that this didn't happen to, regardless of background, education, or net worth. You probably won't notice the first year or maybe even the fifth year. It tends to build up over time.

Think back to over twenty years ago. What were you earning back then? Okay, now freeze that figure, and without any cost-of-living increases, try to make it in the next twenty years. Can't do it, can you? You simply can't hold your breath or tread water that long.

But we don't have to do that. Remember, everything will be paid off, you're eating leftovers, and you have no dry cleaning. But I can't emphasize enough that every time you stand in line or click "buy," it will cost you more.

Let me tell you what else is going to happen that will end up costing you more. Someone will get sick or fall and need long-term care that your insurance won't cover, or you'll find out your coverage is about to be canceled. You might think, *How and why is it that my husband worked for ABC Company for thirty years, and they said they would take care of us, but now they won't?* The why is a new MBA at your precious company who has figured out how to save the company a boatload of money by doing away with your insurance benefits—and he received a bonus for it. The how is you'll be getting a letter in the mail explaining as much. We've seen many letters addressed to good people who can't believe their eyes.

Also, kids are going to call. They're getting a divorce, lost a job, have a large medical expense, need help with school expenses, are about to have their home foreclosed, or have a substance abuse problem. To some degree, you're going to help. You wouldn't be human if you didn't. It will usually be more costly than you anticipated. The good news here is that it will feel good that you're able to lend a hand. Having to say no because you have no other option would make you sick to your stomach.

Remember those graphs and charts that didn't make sense or answer any questions? Think of it this way: some folks use a candle to represent their retirement plan. Picture the candle as representing all of someone's assets, net worth, and income. Upon retirement, a person lights his or her candle and hopes the candle will supply every need, expected and unexpected. He or she hopes the candle will continue to burn at least until he or she dies. There is, of course, no way to replenish the candle. Think back to the conversation about freezing your paycheck for twenty years. How long can you hold your breath?

Of course, it doesn't need to be this way. There is an alternative. Instead of a candle, think of a windmill. Windmills aren't your area of expertise? Well, you are in luck; we're going to spend some time on windmills.

Here in the United States, windmills were originally called wind pumps. They were quite the system in 1854. They're still in use today in rural and arid parts of the country. They're uncomplicated, easy to use, cost-effective, and most importantly, they work really well. Modern technology has not been able to replace them, thank goodness.

Sometimes a windmill draws water from a water source deep underground. The water is moved toward the surface through a pipe that deposits it into a holding tank, trough, pond, or old bathtub.

The vanes at the top of the windmill are what you see spinning on a windy day. This spinning motion powers the mechanical pump that draws the water toward the surface. The ingenious thing about a windmill is that it can replace the water in a holding tank once the water level falls below a desired level. New water is brought to the surface to replace the used or evaporated water.

Another feature of a windmill is a brake that stops the pumping of new water. The brake can be applied when additional water isn't needed. This is a control lever. You turn it off when you don't need it.

So how does this apply to you? Let's think of the windmill as part of your *planning for when*. There are different parts to a windmill, but I'm not going to break down what each part is and its task. Let's just agree that all these parts are working together for you when and how you need water. What's more relevant for us is what is taking place and what the parts represent.

The water that was deposited into the holding tank represents your original principal. You'll be coming to this tank to drink, if you will. You'll need this water in the tank to survive. Some days you'll need more water than other days.

The water you're drinking represents your income needs at this point. I don't care what you're using it for or how much of it you're using. You have no other source, and you don't know how long you're going to need it. You may, however, need it to last several decades.

If you're following me here, you might notice something. Your tank isn't big enough to hold decade's worth of water. You have a limited supply and an unlimited need. It isn't enough water, folks, not for you and not for your smart neighbor.

Go find one of these holding tanks in an arid spot and stare into that tank. By the way, walk there, and you'll get even more of an appreciation for what we're talking about. Walk there, stare into that tank, and say, "That's all I'll ever need. We'll be okay." That would be a very foolish and unwise approach. You shouldn't do it with water, and you shouldn't do it with your income needs.

Let's get back to your windmill. The water needs to be replenished. Your ever-increasing income needs are drawing down your principal. Some of the water also evaporates. This evaporation reflects inflation or cost-of-living increases. We all understand evaporation. Put some water in a container, and set it in the sun. Nature will take care of the rest. Slowly, without you using any of the water, it starts to disappear.

It's the same with your money if you put your money into an account that's designed not to grow in value. Over time, your money will disappear. Over time, what you can purchase with that money is being evaporated. You could put your money in a shoebox, and the same thing would happen. Now, in reality, what often happens is we decide our money doesn't need to grow, and we start using it. Therefore, we have lowered the water level (money) through use and evaporation.

So what's the remedy? Replenish the water, your principal. The water that remains (principal) is getting to a point where it needs to be replaced. At a predetermined level, the water will be pumped into the tank, replenishing your water supply. This replacement is the dividends and interest that your financial planning through investments will pay you, to replace the usage and evaporation (cost-of-living increases). The winds are going to blow, which will power the windmill, which will bring the ever-increasing amounts of needed water (income).

This is just an analogy, but your financial plan should be set up in a similar way to provide income and income replacement.

21

A Good Captain

OKAY, NOW THAT YOU'VE made some real progress, you may still need some help. You need to involve professionals who help to provide solutions. A financial advisor can provide advice and counsel on how to provide for your family. He or she will be important when *planning for when.*

Did you notice I didn't mention which financial products can provide the best solutions? That's because there are a number of ways this can be accomplished, and not everyone's needs or concerns are the same. I'm not here to push a product, but I'll mention one as an example: term life insurance. If you have it you probably don't have enough. There, I said it. Oh, and by the way, it has a cost. Yes, there are costs, and term life insurance is worth multiples of the cost. It provides peace of mind at pennies on the dollar.

Using term life insurance in your *plan for when* will help to provide solutions that aren't available to all people. I've never heard someone say, "We had too much term life insurance" or "I'll never need this much." You're going to need it regardless. Don't fall into the trap of thinking because of your age or economic condition you have no need for term life insurance.

Just so you know, this insurance will probably cost less than those really nice golf clubs, those hunting trips, and even a few months of cable.

A financial professional is like a captain of a ship or plane. You want a solid and reliable vessel, but in a storm, what you really want is an experienced, skilled, and trustworthy captain.

One more item: I've lost count of how many times I've heard, "Aren't financial advisors all the same?" No, they aren't. Let's look at it another way. Let's look to Captain Sully, the airline pilot who successfully landed a passenger plane in the Hudson River without loss of life. Compare that story to those of drunken pilots trying to board planes for flights or ship captains who abandon their ship and passengers after a tragedy, resulting in a huge loss of life.

Not all captains are the same. I'd fly with Capitan Sully anytime.

22

Now What?

I HOPE YOU'VE REALIZED something: you may need to start a plan, update your plan, or trash your existing plan and start over. Whatever the course of action, congratulations are in order! You've realized that a course of action is needed, and now you need to proceed. But how?

The financial services industry has evolved over the last twenty years or so, and that change has led to some positive outcomes that have benefited clients. Individuals and firms recognized the need to provide comprehensive planning and management of clients' needs and that needs vary. Many advisors and firms now have the ability and expertise to address and consolidate the needs of our clients at a single office or firm.

Sometimes the financial services industry is thought of as somewhere to only manage one's investments. Don't get me wrong; this aspect is very important, but it's only part of the overall plan.

How do you go about finding the right advisor to work with? For one, ask friends and acquaintances who they're using. But sometimes the right advisor may contact you first. God forbid. Just take a few minutes to listen to what he or she has to say. You will know quickly if he or she is trying to sell you something or is promising you the moon by simply telling you what you want to hear. My advice is to avoid these people. What you're looking for is someone who will help provide solutions to your needs, some of which you might not be aware of yet.

23

Qualities

WHAT QUALITIES SHOULD YOU look for in an advisor? Let me give you an example. When my wife and I were interviewing a pediatrician for our children, I didn't know how to go about doing such a thing. By word of mouth, my wife found a doctor that she wanted both of us to meet so we could decide if we would entrust our children's care to him. She had been in the medical field, so she had plenty of detailed questions to ask, most of which exceeded my vocabulary and understanding.

The doctor answered the questions to her satisfaction, but more important to me was *how* he went about answering them. He carefully listened to every question and answered them with equal focus. He also brought up questions that we should be asking. All the while he expressed without words that he had no more important place to be than with us, answering our questions and putting together a plan of action for our children's well-being.

I got the impression that our children would be his only patients and his only concern and that he had all the time in the world to address their needs.

I remember one answer to a question that was important to me, something along the lines of "if the children ever needed to be admitted to a local hospital, would you be able to treat them there?" He said, "Should that happen, we would need a specialist with experience and expertise to care for your children. I would monitor their treatment, interact with the specialist, and sit down with you to keep you informed."

Bingo! Doc, you're who we've been looking for! Fifteen years later, we couldn't imagine being with anyone else. By the way, we still feel like we're his only patients. Remember, you need a captain who's able to recognize the need and who has the integrity to follow through.

In your case, the specialists could be experts in family law, estate planning, taxes, complex solutions for a family-owned business, mortgage needs—in short, a team to work with your primary financial advisor.

Pick those who will tell you what you need to hear, not necessarily what you want to hear. This "something" may be a subject you're well aware of but have not yet addressed. Or it may be something you're not aware of. You don't want to hire a "yes" person. You're in search of a trusted advisor who will confirm all the good and bring up needed topics, even if they might be a little uncomfortable to discuss. He or she will be looking out for your best interest and putting your well-being first.

Planning for When
A Woman's Guide to Financial Planning

Why financial planning is important to you and your family.

How to become an active participant in planning and how to find
people to assist you as you *plan for when*.

Kevin W. Pinkley

About the Author

Kevin Pinkley and Wealth Management Group are located in Houston. They provide strategies in financial planning, retirement planning, concentrated wealth, and corporate planning to clients in Texas and numerous other states.

Kevin has earned the Accredited Investment Fiduciary Analyst designation, Certified Investment Management Analyst designation, and Certified Divorce Financial Analyst credentials.